PAMP~LE~MOUSSE

Vol. 4, No. 3

PAMPLEMOUSSE

Vol. 4, No. 3

Editors
Louis LoRe, Alex Vetere, Ashley Slayton, Josh Cardosi, Cole Shebak

Faculty Advisors
Jensen Beach & Elizabeth Powell

Design Editor
Adam Robinson

Cover Photo
Isaiah Perry

Pamplemousse, formerly known as *The Gihon River Review*, published biannually, was founded in the fall of 2001 as a production of the BFA program at Johnson State College. Starting in the Fall of 2010, its production became based in a Literary Publishing class offered at the college by the BFA program, conducted by Professors Elizabeth A.I. Powell and Jensen Beach. Pamplemousse publishes high quality, forward thinking, innovative, and well-crafted writing in many genres and styles. We relish discovering new voices, as well as featuring established favorites.

Issues are $7 each. Submissions in poetry, fiction, graphic fiction, nonfiction, and art are read from September to May. Poetry submissions may not exceed five poems; fiction and nonfiction may not exceed twenty-five pages. Please visit our website, pamplemoussevt.org to submit using our submissions manager.

CONTENTS

LISA TADDEO

BLUE WRECK

1

It was nearing dark when the Amish girl knocked her tiny fist against his door. Woody knew it was her because it was the knock of a virgin.

He opened the door and smiled. Her trusting face framed by a white bonnet. Behind her shoulders silos rose vigorously against the skid-marked sky.

She carried a burlap sack of dusty potatoes and some gems of garlic. There was even a wet bottom shoo fly pie, in a canvas tote he was meant to give back.

"Come in, Patience," he said.

She was plain and ageless—eleven, twelve, Mona Lisa. Her face was the color of a candle. But there was a humanity to the child he never saw anymore, not even in her self-sacrificing tribe.

Woody went to refrigerate the pie and set the sack down on the Formica table. A couple of potatoes tumbled out. Sprouts emanated from the spuds like strong white worms.

When he returned, she was petting the dog from head to rump.

"May I?" she asked, taking a biscuit from her pocket. He liked to think of her as his own, but a natural child wouldn't ask permission to give the dog a treat. He didn't answer so she put the biscuit back in her pocket.

"Will your people wait until the morning to find out?"

Patience thought for a moment and nodded.

From his torso he produced an oceanic noise. "Well if curiosity gets the better of you, you come back down here." He pointed to his television set. "We'll be up until the fat lady sings."

The child smiled warmly. Her mother was not this tender. It always surprised him, the way children became their own people. He looked out his door, down the purple dirt road.

"I suppose it's useless to ask if you want a ride."

She nodded again and cast her eyes in the direction of home.

"You thank your ma for me," he said, and closed the door.

He took a Keystone from the fridge, noting the cold molasses pond on the middle shelf. Diane used to sponge the shelves weekly. Stuck half her body in there to pursue the corners. From behind, she looked like a babysitter. That nice big ass in blue jeans. He'd come up behind it quietly, pretending it wasn't his.

Stella watched Woody watch the screen. She was a black Lab, full of face but not overweight. Diane used to say to the dog, Quit looking at me. You're fed, exercised. Go about your night.

Woody didn't mind. Only a dog could watch you like that, make you not feel watched.

He sunk his kidneys into the recliner and pulled the waistband of his sweats down, letting the rolls unpack themselves. In a sense his weight gain—forty pounds in under a year—felt like a success. A victory of the flesh, of the aspiration of cells to multiply without restraint. Like Diane's cancer, murmured Corporal Buttons, remotely.

On his way home he'd stopped at the fire station where the volunteers ate pepperoni pizza and laughed. He was meant to hand his ballot to a young Filipino girl in pigtails. She had her palms out for it. The smell of the pizza was rosy and everyone seemed to have plans for the weekend.

Corporal Buttons was the last time Woody had felt known. He'd met the Corporal on a cross country train trip, after 9/11 when he'd become afraid to fly. Woody was on the Zephyr to Emeryville, where Diane was undergoing an experimental surgery. Her pedophilic uncle Dudley Nine Fingers knew someone who knew someone and the smooth bastard was paying for it, too.

On the first evening of the trip Woody sat in the dining car. He ordered the roast chicken with rosemary and carrots, plus a glass of red wine. A gentleman strode in like a gust of winter, wearing a Civil War shell jacket.

"Mind if I sit?"

Woody had looked down the length of the car. All the tables were empty. Without waiting for an answer the man distributed himself across the banquette. From the fibers of his clothes a great dust rose up—an airy talc of crushed moths—followed by a silver stink. Woody stifled a cough.

Some people are either born with the gift of unobtrusiveness or they are ghosts, and nobody finds out until the end.

The announcer on the television tonight reminded him of Rite-Aid Rita, the same enticing red hair and mouth. The same sense that you could plunge your middle age into this broad, a black hole of mothering. They had two nice Saturdays. On the third one she cried like a savage thing in his bed. Her fingernails tore at the covers. He smoked a cigarette for the first time since the war, staring up at the quiet insects in the glass of the ceiling light.

He watched CNN because it had been Diane's channel. Two hours after the polls closed, the East was remade into land banks of blue.

He walked into the bedroom. Stella followed. She always did if he poked in there too early. The marijuana was with the gun, the former wrapped in a plastic baggie, the latter nude and toy-like. Side by side in his bad boy drawer. He still thought of it that way, well into his sixties.

Back on the couch he packed a pipe and snuffled the bright pong of marijuana. Sunset-colored hairs on furred green leaves. Diane's medical leftovers, named *Blue Wreck* on the plastic tube. He fired the bowl, sucked it deep and kept it inside of himself, letting his lungs and brain and blood absorb the maximum concentration of smoke. When Diane smoked she'd never done so lustily. She smoked like she ate, sensibly chewing rectangles of pork chop, neat corners of yolk-wetted toast. Unlike Rite-Aid Rita, who applied everything to her lips the same phallic way. Shapes of all kinds galloped into Rita's mouth. He aspired to miss it.

On the television men in suits were talking about the Rust Belt. They said the phrase so often and so suddenly that it began to sound foolish and insincere.

"Here I am, boys," said Woody, holding his Keystone up to the screen.

The house—a shabby white Colonial with slanted linoleum floors, counters warped with burns—was in the middle of Lancaster County, down a dirt road with dog-sized ruts. He and Diane used to live in Johnstown, 170 miles to the west, where he'd worked at the mill for thirty plus years. This place had been his family's. When his mother passed, a quick five months after Diane—as though the old bag had been waiting just long enough to outlive her—Woody moved in. Took the job at Qdoba to stave off idle hands. But otherwise he'd begun decomposing. He didn't floss. Hadn't washed the quilt. It smelled of his mother still, yellow flowers and toes.

But it was beautiful at sunset in the middle of nothing. It was as though America spread her legs, in the birthing sense. As evening approached the boom of trucks ranged to the wings of the earth; down the center came the darkening corn and the roving birds and the freshly-minted moon.

Now the marijuana hunger cored a gorge down his middle. He opened a can of Ro-tel and a can of Goya black beans. He poured the beans out into a bowl, then gently shook the Ro-tel over them. He was always trying to empty the cabinets. He had too much of the staples, on account of the big box store. The cruelty of a family pack. Bean cans by the dozen. Enough cream of wheat to last him longer than he meant to live.

On the television the red-haired woman said, "Fasten your seatbelts, kiddoes, it's going to be a bumpy night."

"Dog," Woody called. Stella's eyes activated. "Come sit up here beside me." He tapped the couch and she cocked her fat dark head and licked the air. She came and lay beside his feet.

By two in the morning it was clear who would win.

He ate the shoo fly pie with his hands and drifted off to sleep, his fingers vulgar with confection.

2

In the morning Woody delivered a Mexican breakfast to a baseball diamond on the iffy side of town. The sun shone as orange and American as ever. As he approached the field he saw it was a group of kids with Down syndrome playing pretend-softball. They wore green caps that said Coventry Peaceful Friends Academy and were miming the plays, ball-less but content. Behind the batter's box, a trio of women teachers were chatting and watching the children, their faces calm as clocks.

Stella was in the car for all deliveries. He brought her out and the kids dropped their mitts and rushed like an ocean. *What type of dog is it. What's his name. Does he bite. Is he named Rover? My dog is named Rover.*

He was proud of Stella. As he'd been of Diane. They were his black beauties, and he'd treated them like extensions of himself, sending them out into the world like bold tentacles. At night he would suck them back into his chest, looking across what they'd seen and heard.

One little ginger-haired girl brought her nose right up to Stella's. She stayed that way for a long while. A boy in corduroy overalls said, "What are you doing, Minnie?"

"Dogs can see inside you," she said, "when they look in your eyes. I'm letting this nice doggie see my ideas."

The child was beautiful. The eyes were a glittering sea green. Her coloring complemented her condition. Stella licked the girl's nose and she giggled. She looked at Woody and said, "Her breath is not bad."

One of the teachers approached. Woody felt that anybody who took care of such children was a good person. The woman was heavily-freckled and wore a shapeless blue skirt. Before and after Diane he'd seen women through the lens of the positions from which they would suit him best. This one, he figured, he would roll sideways. During Diane he hadn't thought like that at all, or just barely.

"I'm so sorry," she said as he handed her the foil-lined bag of breakfast burritos, "we just realized we don't have enough for tip." She thrust a rolled-up newspaper towards him. It was *The New York Times*, which he had only seen once or twice up close.

"Want this?" she asked. "We bought thirty copies. In case it's worth something."

He nodded, and his face got hot. He wrangled Stella from the children and got back in the car. The little redheaded child was waving as he drove off.

He parked in the The Bullfrog's lot and ate his lunch. He was sick of Mexican. At the same time, it was the only thing he could think to eat. No matter what he did, he found himself every day at noon, forking rice and beans and cool wet meat into his mouth.

He'd seen the Qdoba job on a bulletin board at the Weis Market.

Freedom to be yourself. Drive your own car. Listen to your own tunes. Get paid to spread some flavor love. Interested? Yup, we thought so.

He did listen to music and accessed his bank of memories. At stoplights he got lost in waves of auburn hair, his fingers caught in sprayed sections of up-do.

One night during the war with a whore named Cam. She didn't want money, only to go to dinner. They ate at a bar in Saigon, prawns in a steaming garlic broth. She was lithe and excitable, and their relations were more balancing act than intercourse.

Shortly after coming home there was Linda from the neighborhood. Not a perfect body by any means or any sort of brain to work with but she was happier to see him than his own mother.

Maura Penny, the only woman he went away with before Diane, to a bed and breakfast out by Jamestown, called 1801 House. Maura Penny, who got undressed like a hot potato coming out of its skin. They sat in the basement of the place, an empty honor bar with original stone walls and oak beams, bottles of liquor from other centuries and cherry candle wax on chess tables. They licked a bottle of Noyau de Poissy and danced to Julio Iglesias. *POY-see*, Maura hummed in his ears and the morning came faster than had all the ones before.

Why, he wondered, were the good times always marked by women? Oh formidable poon, dark and barnlike.

He flipped through the fancy paper and came across an ad for an apartment building. In a room of light wood and a surplus of windows that nobody deserved, a woman in a long black dress with dark hair gathered tightly and dripping earrings looked on as her muscled husband swam in a slate pool, suspended over the city. The Empire State Building was heaven-lit in the background. They were probably the best looking couple he had ever seen. Of course, Woody knew those were just models.

His younger brother worked in Manhattan with lots of those lost, sexy souls. His brother, in a sense, had gotten out. Out of what, the fuck did he know. Sometimes when Mac called, he was in a wonderful mood. He was floating. Other times he was distant. The son, after all.

In their family tree there was a gaping hole where the branches of good fortune should extend. Nothing had ever been equitable for longer than a night of his life. It was more than just being born into the right country or the right family. It was more than money. Though of course these things were part of it.

See his brother, who had moved away. Escaped the muddle of low-class folks trying to keep each other down. Mac married a good-enough girl from their hometown and smoothed her out and got himself a computer job in Manhattan. But the first kid was born retarded. When Woody heard the news—and this would have been after his own loss— deep down he felt a terrible sunburst, thinking that he himself couldn't have done anything differently to have a better life. That it was in their genes. Deeper down than their genes, it was something blackening the earth at their feet. They crawled along fault lines. They sowed their seed in rot. It was in the water. It was in the starless breath of his mother. It was in the fortune cookie he got when he was thirteen years old. *A cheerful message is on its way to you.*

The next morning he'd found his old man dead in the yard. He'd shot himself by the clothesline where the family's pants skipped in the wind.

3

After clocking out in the afternoon, Woody drove out to the town where the young professionals were closing in on the farmers, and the farm-stands had begun to sell specialty pastas and gourmet olive oils and six olives in a single glass jar. He was going to get the maple pecan stone-ground chocolate that Patience loved.

The farmstand attracted a certain breed. Everything was overpriced. Fresh chickens with organic scrotums. What the fuck was kohlrabi.

There was mulled cider. The first set of Christmas trees was being unloaded. The smell of fir was crisp and aching.

Two women, with three straw children between their protracted legs, presided over parsnips and purple carrots and rutabagas. The crackly radio played, "Beast of Burden."

"We are reeling," said the tall blond. "We won't stop reeling. It's a new reality. It's a surreal reality and a dangerous one."

"Yes," said the brunette. "John is staying home from work today. I threw up in the middle of the night, after Wisconsin."

"Paul went to work, but only to show solidarity. He's the team leader now."

"I meant to ask you," said the brunette, "how was the Farm Dinner?"

"Oh, God, it feels like a different era," said the blond. "And it was only last week! I saw all these people, whites and African Americans and the Urdu family with the girl with the cleft lip? It was a really nice community event. Black and white, gay and straight, young and old, eating local food, talking around a bonfire. The America I know and love, the America I will fight for." She raised an elegant fist. "Fight, fight, fight," she said, weakly.

"It's the little things," agreed the brunette.

The little things, indeed. What would Corporal Buttons say to these women, thought Woody, about the little things.

Now Corporal Buttons was not the man's name. Woody never learned his name, but he'd been wearing that jacket with the gold sleeve braid indicating rank and two rows of brass buttons, each one different. Most of them featured the eagle, but some were marked O for Ordnance, some A for Artillery, and Engineer and Infantry and Cavalry ones.

Woody had spoken at length with Corporal Buttons about how he felt with Dudley paying. But it was the only chance they had.

"No shame in it," said Corporal Buttons. He looked out the train window with his white hands clasped.

"But there is. This man stuck his hands in my woman, and more, when she was young."

"He deserves to pay, then."

Something lifted off of Woody. Funny that words from a stranger could cool you down like a rain.

"There's more," Woody said, and the older man looked at him. "I feel I'm at confession." He told the old man everything. There'd been a child. They hadn't named her. She'd lived for fourteen days, misshapen and huge-eyed, a skinned crow. Just once they bathed it—her—in a clear plastic tub in the hospital. What he remembered most was the scared red neck. Though they'd been advised against contamination, Diane took her infant's hand in her mouth. The nurse left the room.

"You did a good thing," said Corporal Buttons. "To give life is to give back."

They'd told them, with enough time to humanely handle things, that the baby would be born damaged. It would have a small chance of living through the first week. He'd seen the fear in Diane's eyes, and somehow that fear had made him want to puff up.

He placed his palm against his woman's sloped stomach. "We'll keep our child," he said to the doctor and Diane. And it wasn't about politics or religion. It was something lower and less dependable.

Then came the dog. A dog that saved his life more than once. One time when his old girlfriend had come to the house. She'd worn boots that came up above her knees and brought a flask monogrammed with her late husband's initials. It was shortly after the death of the child and Diane was at her mother's. Woody reasoned that it was just about surviving by the hour. But he didn't do anything and it was the dog that stopped him. A low growl filled the room like thunder. The black eyes gleamed. Woody had to tell the woman to go. That's when he knew she was bad news. A woman who would have stayed through the growl of a beast—she was clearly a cripple.

"You did good," said the Corporal. His voice was distant and gruff. He said the things Woody's father had never said, would not have said even if he had stuck around for all the subsequent nightmares.

Back then the train sighed to a stop in Kalispell. Woody looked out at the men in hats on the track. I could be a cowboy, he thought, if she dies. If she dies, I will return to Montana and I will deal in cows and eat perpetual steak and find a woman who will nurse me with her giant tits.

Now Woody made inadvertent eye contact with the blond. She was filling a brown sack with glistening butter lettuce. He looked away. You couldn't so much as glance at an attractive lady without her thinking you wanted her. He hadn't shaven in two days. He used to look good unshaven; Diane liked him best with what she called a nine o'clock shadow. Now he merely looked homeless and old. The other broad looked him up and down and hissed, Fucking *racists*.

The blond said, "Oh thank *God* the tom tom tomatoes are back! Have you had these!"

He realized he may have just imagined the racist line. Regardless, they hated him. They hated him and were indifferent at the same time. The only way to exist in this ever-narrowing world, for a man like Woody, was to sit on the stoop and chew his own heart like it was jerky.

Underfoot, Stella whined. It sounded mutinous and he nearly kicked her. Corporal Buttons was quiet but revolutionary in his large, hairy ears.

4

At home Woody positioned the chocolates in the Mae West catch-all by the door, next to the tin the pie had been in. He wished the child would come tonight. If she didn't come by four o'clock, the odds that she'd come at all were small. After checking his Lucky 4 Life numbers and being just two shy, he realized he wanted the child to come more than he wanted to win the lottery. Stella was lying on her side, which meant nobody was around for at least a half mile.

Stella could smell saliva in a brook, she could smell illness before illness had chosen its host. When it first came for Diane, it wasn't a low throb or a bright billy club, it wasn't pain at all but a grayness that dimmed the lamps of her eyes. The worst things always come from the sides. For months before Diane complained of anything, Stella laid at her feet every night. Idiotically, the two of them never questioned the dog's new behavior.

Some time later a nurse practitioner who said she was an avid reader jacked a wrist inside of his wife's canal, waggled it like a periscope, clutched around and said, Has anyone ever told you you have a fibroidy uterus?

In the delivery car and out in the world he tried to keep his thoughts on baseball. Pizza. Poker. He thought about the minor women. The Jessicas and Barbaras and all their erotic knees.

But in the privacy of his home, he would think only of Diane. Right then, he was recalling the barbecue they'd gone to at a friend's house, in the first year of their love. Diane drank rum and cokes and he drank bourbon. By the end of the night he had gotten into a fight with Rod Healy, both of them drunk and crushed out like cans on the lawn.

"It's our anniversary," Diane whispered in his ear. He remembered she'd worn a yellow dress with a darker yellow belt. Her waist was small and her hips were not. She was the prettiest woman he'd ever seen, any-where. Certainly on that lawn.

"Anniversary of what?" he asked, and she whispered in his ear and touched her boiling tongue to the underside of the lobe.

Diane would have loved it here. The wholesome red barns, the great snaking rivers of lime, even the power lines like robot scarecrows polic-ing the fields. Every time she'd come here in the past she hated it, on account of his mother. Now it would just have been him and her and the dog. Eating deep orange yolks and bacon. The dog romping while they sipped peach lemonade in the summer and drank egg nog and whisky in the winter. It was almost Christmastime. Where does a man go who has made no children. He would not go by Mac's. He was sadder every time after.

He smoked a bowl and then, for the first time, ate one of the mari-juana jolly ranchers. It smelled like weed, it was glossy and the taste was the kind that made the back of his teeth itch for more. He'd abstained during the war. He was always going around saying he didn't want his senses impaired. Now all he wanted was to become impaired. Unman-ageably so.

Towards the end, Diane wanted that, too. It hurt his feelings because he was a child.

The last few months the marijuana was the only thing that made her eat, that kept them both sane. Does it hurt, he asked every day and, How much? She tapped his wrist. Don't take this from me, too, she said.

He spent a lot of time during the run-up to the end, trying to analyze how much of his sorrow was for what she would miss out on in life, good St. Louis ribs and their own lovemaking, versus how much was his own agony and fear of abandonment. Diane used to say that useless people cried for themselves and not for the dying.

He got off that train in Emeryville. He'd been so filled with desire to see her that, by the time the bell dinged, he flew out without saying goodbye to Corporal Buttons, who'd gone for a siesta in his cabin.

As Woody was walking to her room, Dudley was coming towards him, plus two nurses with short legs and long faces.

"We lost her," said Dudley. "We goddamned fucking lost her."

Woody thought of which city he'd been in the moment it happened. He thought of the pervert holding her hand. The nurses she didn't know. The paint job on the ceiling, the wattage of bulb she'd looked upon and the exact cast of the light in the room as the emerald breath was drawn.

It had been just outside of Denver, in any case, where Corporal Buttons told him that each button on his jacket was plucked off the chest of a different man he'd killed.

It's the little things, he'd said. Which made Woody think of the way the cubed flesh and bread crumbs gathered around Diane's gold wedding band when she was forming meatballs. The way that afterwards, she rinsed her hands under scalding water. Only a real woman could rinse her hands under scalding water, and not flinch.

It had taken an hour or so but his body had begun to vibrate with the drug. His veins felt ticklish and the blood in all his limbs sunk towards the floor.

Getting high didn't make him feel light. It made him see the truth. In this place, Woody was not the victim but the monster. If people think that's what you are, then that's what you'll stay. At first Diane had tried to impart upon him how to live in the world. She gave him books—James Baldwin and Arthur Herman—with meaningful passages underlined. No matter how he raged, she remained steady.

And how did he repay her? By killing her. By making her bear that child. The doctors said no, of course not, no way no how. But deep down he knew.

Diane had wanted to name the baby. The name she'd chosen was Stella. She'd crocheted a pillow with the name Stella in buttery cursive. It ended up above the non-working fireplace. Last month, Woody brought it down from the mantle and gave it to the dog. She carried it around in her mouth and didn't harm it.

He turned on the television. There were protests in New York City, white women wearing sombreros and holding artistic signs.

He was happy they didn't win. For once they wouldn't get to go around, flapping their gums. They were all like the doctors in the room when Diane died. It was a teaching hospital and the room was full of young men and women. One small Asian resident had shaken her head from side to side, marveling. Interesting case! she said.

They didn't understand, it wasn't about race or money, but about the living and the dying. They didn't understand men like Woody, who had always been on the side of the dying. You didn't get to go around the way they did, not forever.

The way, for example, the women at the farmstand looked at him, and looked at Stella, as though they thought she was unfortunate for having him as an owner. And what they'd called him! Maybe not to his face, but in their worsted little hearts.

What did any of them know, the hell they had to go through. He'd renounced his own mother. He didn't see her again, from the day she'd called Diane that name, until the day Patience's mother sent word. He sped down highway 41, because it was still his mother. The Amish woman opened the door for him to his childhood home, flour-cheeked and void of judgment, and pointed to the bedroom. His mother was cool as a doll. Her teeth were in water on the prim, cheap nightstand. The lace doily was suddenly ridiculous. Everything she had ever tended was now nothing.

Now the weed had sunk beneath even the veins, thrumming like a school of fish inside the bones. He got the spins and put both arms out like wings to steady himself, although he was already sitting.

He looked at Stella. Sonofabitch. She had torn a hole in Diane's pillow.

Was she one of them? He wasn't sure. Certainly nobody left was one of him.

The other week he found his bar of soap had a stratum of shit around the middle. He scratched at it with his fingernail, smelled his fingers. Jesus. Caked in there. Actual *shit*. The whole world was sticking it to him.

He went into the bedroom. The drawer was open. He hadn't closed it after removing the jolly rancher. He brought out his father's gun, polished it with the hem of his large shirt. The bedspread was the color of cola. There drapes were the color of algae. His mother had such rotten taste. Why had he even for a moment worried that she had a reason to spurn his wife?

Stella was looking inside his eyes. It was true that she could see inside. Straight to the rot at the back of his throat.

Do it, said Corporal Buttons, in his ear hole. She's a traitor. Every single last shit of them is.

He sat down on the couch. He shook his head at the dog. The pillow in her mouth, the stuffing coming out like a portion of cloud.

Do it, said Corporal Buttons. Kill the bitch.

Woody tried to shoot the dog between the eyes, but it went off to the left a little. It was so quick there was no cry. Her muscular body became baggy and her back slumped heavily against the wall, the four legs surrendering forward. At the bottom of the lolling snout, the silky black gums curved into what appeared to be a grin. It was such a ridiculous sight that, for a long time, he wouldn't believe it was real.

DONNA PUCCIANI

BLUEBERRIES

Gathered by hand from a bush
in Indiana, rinsed and dried,
nested in the freezer,
they witness a deep friendship
over decades and state lines.

They come to us humbly,
without pretensions, here
in the shadow of skyscrapers
in Chicago, a granite city
on the Lake.

They carry with them
a purple warmth, a woody
scent stirred into batter, the loaf
of a February day, in a kitchen
that remembers the bond

between people, between
things of the earth and the flesh
of humans who pick, wash,
bag and share, who eat
of a dark communion,

who carry a spare slice
across the street for neighbors,
the stains of affection,
the crumbs of something
hallowed that no politician,

even on a blue Monday,
a frozen Tuesday,
even on a moonless night
or the sunless days of winter,
can take away.

TRYING TO REMEMBER

Remembering spring
is almost impossible,
like remembering youth,
the days when walking
was never a chore,

or breathing. Photographs
witness both seasons,
rendering the knowledge
of birdsong, rainfall,
and a well-oiled shoulder.

The tuneless chirps
remind us of the days
when relatives could see us off
at the airport, when
one job was enough.

The birds have returned
to make us hear their inevitable
hymns to dawn. Snowdrops
come uninvited, with rabbits
to eat their sad white buds.

Give thanks even for times
that disappear quickly
in the rear-view mirror
of the old Toyota, never to return,
for laugh-lines multiplying
on an unrecognizable face.

KEN HAAS

AMERICAN SUSHI

A pescetarian friend tells me fish are fair eating
because they don't form relationships. Which he knows
from having read that their tendency to school is mere
genetic radar. So his passion for sushi is legitimate,
though he bemoans its Americanization and
points out that we stole it not too long after winning WWII
with the A-Bomb—brought it first to Hollywood as a fad.
Now it's in Walgreens; there's a California Academy
of Sushi, chefs who never go to market, restaurants
with boats of *nigiri* that circle on conveyor belts
offering species on the verge of extinction.
He just doesn't see the Philadelphia roll,
stuffed with cream cheese of all things,
as the product of a democratic society;
rather, as the colonization of a holy cuisine,
which he indulges in once a week on Thursday evenings,
using only his fingers to dip only the fish slice,
not the vinegared rice, in the soy sauce,
which is how he says they do it in Japan,
where he has never been.
He relates with reverence
the *itamae's* precise hand pressure,
the sharpness of the knives, the fumy bamboo mats—
how this began as a food of the people
back when freshly caught tuna
had to be stored in fermenting rice to keep from spoiling,
how each fish has its own spirit which must be honored
much like the Navajo used to apologize to the buffalo.
My friend dreams of rolling into the Taste of Tokyo

on Wall Street, demonstrating how to eat without consuming,
freeing the souls of the *maguro, ikura, tako,* and *unagi*
from the cruel and sloppy hunger of the local princes.

CONTACT LENSES
FOR CHICKENS

A Harvard Business School case in the '70s proposed
inserting purposely clouded contacts into the furtive eyes
of chickens to boost farm profits by curbing hostile pecking
and cannibalism—those historical drags on egg production.

A few entrepreneurs did give it a go. And the science
actually panned out, led to more manageable workers,
though the business model pretty much sucked—
contractors who regularly visited farms for other reasons
weren't sufficiently dexterous or disposed
to try and shove the darn things into the peepers
of livestock descendant from velociraptors.

Ideas that fail in one context, though, can thrive in another.
Perhaps we should try special lenses on human chickens:
Those afraid of the dark get contacts with night vision.
Afraid of frogs and you get green ones—can't tell a toad
from the innocent grass. Have a heightened fear of crowds
and you get fractals—see the world one thug at a time.
Phobic about intimacy and we'll prescribe a pair like
the side views on cars—objects appear farther than they are.

And, for those who aren't chicken enough, contacts
like the warped mirrors in amusement parks
that make everything look larger, including the balls of
the chicken across the street or across the ocean to whom
we sold the gun and lenses that make everything look small.

ON BEING SLAPPED BY A WOMAN I DON'T KNOW

Intermission at the Opera. Saturday night.
All I know about her is the pageboy cut
of raven red hair. She stands abruptly
then uses the full arc of her body turn
to imprint the left side of my face.
One contact lens now lodged up under its eyelid,
a bicuspid stuck to the inside of my mouth,
my cheek like a pup tent smacked by lightning.
I had never been slapped by a woman before—
though there was something about it I missed.
Bacall giving it to Bogie. Crawford to Gable.
Deserved. Delivered. On to the next scene.
Black and white. Though mine seemed technicolor.
Turns out she had been twirling one tip
of her reading glasses between her front teeth
while the other tip was tickling her ear.
Which she thought was me, from the row behind,
flirting or trying to filch one of her diamond studs.
Probably some other guy had earned it.
Or I had earned it elsewhere.
Edging my hand under Faye Brown's impossible bra,
her dad glued to *Gunsmoke* downstairs.
Teasing my ex-wife for airballing a foul shot
in front of twenty thousand fans during halftime
at the Oakland Coliseum on taco night.
Asking my mom, just before heading off to college,
why she let her kids be strapped
and what she got out of watching.

I was a good boy once.
May have been an okay man.
Though the heart never believes this.
Needs a sharp reset. A briskly wiped slate.
That's what I missed. The clarity.
And the wakeup doesn't hurt much,
requires no response.
Just blink a few times, wiggle the jaw,
welcome rough justice.
The curtain is rising.
Carmen is taking her mark.

SEVERANCE PAY

My father believed
the toughest part of his job
was to be the toughest part of me.

To whip me for my own good
into a chip gouged
from the old concrete block
that the SS couldn't bow,
Kamikazes couldn't cow,
dog years at the gear face couldn't own.

To spoon-feed me his gut and heart
that wouldn't quit.
And never did.

In the end
it was the artery between them
that pumped to a purple boil,
then blew,
strained as the bond between
vampire twins vying for the same blood.

       When I see him in dreams
he asks is there no chance anymore
for these two sorry soldiers,
with adverse takes on courage,
still unsure if they asked of each other
too much or too little.

And I tell him
it's the yoke not the link
that's been undone,
so they're talking all the time these days,
just as we are now.

THE WORK OF LUCK

The Powerball jackpot sits at $700 million,
and I still won't play. A quant nerd once told me
my chances of winning were statistically the same
whether I bought a ticket or not.
Which at first I thought was a math joke.
Then figured she might be pointing out
that there's no measurable difference between
trying to buy one's way into fortune and finding
that one-in-a-zillion ticket soaked in the gutter.
Or maybe she was saying no one's that lucky.
It's all a hoax like astronauts landing on the moon.

But none of that's why I've never indulged.
I was born white, in this country, in this slice
of human history, not before or after.
If there's a limit to luck, I've crossed it.
Dirty Harry shot me with a .44 Magnum
and the bullet caromed off my nose.
I should be ashamed to seek any more blessing.
Though I'm not.

Perhaps it's the well-documented curse of luck.
The SuperLotto champs whose lives it ruined.
46-year-old Chicagoan who dropped dead
the day after—poisoned by his sister-in-law;
Philly woman who scored twice in five years
then each time blew it all in Atlantic City—
overdosed on heroin in a storage locker.
Impressive. But not enough to have stopped me

from taking a shot at the even better life.

No, I have to blame the reluctance on my mother.
And her mother. And hers. And hers. And hers.
God knows what happened to them in Babylon
and Seville. I know about Deutschland.

They whisper every day directly into my brain,
from a place where every bet is already settled,
that they didn't buy me all this luck so I could
go to the opera, work on a suntan,
pretend everyone born has an equal play,
live life as though if only I had more then
I would try to do something about the future.

SCOTT LAUDATI

MY SUITCASE IS PACKED

I know you're home out there
in Colorado where the desert flowers
wait all year to turn yellow
and horses with Spanish blood
whip their manes under lightning
as the snows melt down to refill
the dried beds. Enough was enough
and you had to put a continent
between me and New Jersey.
I've seen that land and pulled over
to swim naked where the white crests
shatter freedom, which is something more
than no dead ends on your streets.
The rain falls straight down
and even stray cats
come when they're called.
I bled for you once
when the war was still far from over,
and the end hasn't gotten any closer.

THE LAST STREETLIGHT
IN HEAVEN

I hope the boys can use their track marks
as road maps and hold the hands of girls
who sold their final sacrament
on the Newark streets,
where spring feels like December
where glass clogs the gutter
and no price is too high
for a whole generation to erase
some of its hunger.

These towns flood now,
but the rains never come.
There are enough mother's tears
to water the lawns. And every man's
poverty contains the origin of night.
The absence of god is the first syringe.
We were a town once,
but nothing is left: There's no sky
clear enough for the lucky ones
to reckon under a whole history
of past sins built above Indian bones.

The interest keeps rising on
America's crimes. Our parents lined up to vote
and hoped it would always stay the same.
The hurricane comes and the shattered
glass gets washed away,
and they keep signing up fresh faces.

LINDA ELFERS-MABLI

SPRING CLEAN-UP

Half-buried, a diminutive skull,
with deep eye sockets,
a jaw locked open in pain lay
in a cradle of overgrown ivy and periwinkle.

Remnants of a lost battle with a mangy fox
ripping through fur and sinew
while the August sun seared the corpse,
leaving nothing behind but blanched bones.

I witnessed the carnage safely
from my kitchen window,
quickly returning to dish washing. And then
the spring thaw, revealed my callousness

once again as I raked away
dead leaves, brittle twigs, and rabbit bones.

HOUSE FOR SALE

Clutching my arms, I defend myself
from shivering. No frigid mist from my mouth -
just a wintery wave swirling like a floating icy cape.

Around my bare feet, blueish purple lotuses reveal
their golden prickly centers in time lapse progression,
spurting their intoxicating honey fragrance.
A staircase to rooms shuttered; musty air, stale mood.
Chill clings like a petulant child.

I wade through lotus petals turning pale, shriveling
from the cold radiating from my body.
Numbing calm, eyes fluttering,
muscles melt through floor planks,
          dripping through the basement ceiling,
                    down the knot-hole wood paneling,
                              penetrating cement floor cracks,
back to the cold dirt of early spring

A GIRL WALKS INTO A BAR

4:31pm PST

Quinn is lost in the casino. But she likes being lost, in the arousing glow of the slot machines, amid the steady rattle of ice in highball glasses and game-show white noise. She knows that she is lost in a deeper sense, as well—in a way she can't quite pinpoint. But she doesn't want to look for herself. She's afraid of what she might find.

She spots her friends in the lounge, standing with a group of men. No one would call her friends "women." They are plainly girls. They have that fresh out of college aura. Quinn has a youthful glow that allows her to traipse into a place like this with damp hair and a denim jacket without anyone calling her out on it. Her friends are neither damp nor denim-clad. They are polished, false-lashed and blown dry. She is the quirky one. She knows quirky is a kinder word for weird, but she'll take it. Quirky Quinn. A misfit among oddballs and squares alike.

"You're *late*!" the girls are howling. "Lost again?"

"In a good way," she replies.

"This is Brad," her friend Jessica says, gesturing to one of the men. "It's Brad's bachelor party. Brad's getting married!"

"Ah," she says. Which means: *No need to waste my time here, then.*

"Marriage is a joke," a hulking figure in a blazer interjects. He spills a splash of whiskey onto her toes, but she doesn't flinch. Her toes were made for foreign liquids, to be stomped on at concerts, to be stubbed against walls.

"What are you drinking," she asks, "and why don't I already have one in my hand?"

The man guides her to the bar. "What do you really want?"

"Red Bull and vodka. And for you to tell me why you hate marriage so much. Are you divorced?"

"Not divorced," he says, flagging down the bartender and slurring her drink order. "Not divorced, just fucking pissed."

Quinn scans the man like he's a mannequin in a window, that same way men scan women, searching for whatever. What she finds is this: handsome, like network TV crime-procedural detective handsome. What she wants is this: Godfather-era Al Pacino handsome. But she'll take this! She wouldn't dare be picky-choosy. This is Las Vegas. This is the kind of petri dish of amorality a girl like Quinn thrives in.

"Let's talk about something else," she suggests.

"Do you have a boyfriend?" he asks.

"Excellent question. You can ask me *anything*, and that's what you want to know."

"I need to know if you're off-limits," he says, more lascivious than chivalrous. "You're the kind of girl that drives me crazy. The kind of girl that's cute and knows she's cute and doesn't need anyone to tell her."

Quinn slurps her drink through the straw. It's down to the ice. "You're totally misreading me," she says. "I live for validation."

She hands him her glass and glances toward the bartender, and Blazer Man gives her this look like, another already?

Until women are making at least 90 cents on the dollar, she is not going to buy her own drinks.

"I don't have a boyfriend," she tells him as they shuffle back to the group. It's a motley crew of thirty-somethings who, with the exception of Brad the Bachelor, all remain nameless, all milling about in their blue button-ups like they're at a conference. There is a desperate need for nametags in this place. Who organized this? If Quinn could have her way, they'd be playing spin the bottle in some dingy dive. This is too formal. The pretense is drowning them. She doesn't get the point of pretense when everyone wants the same thing, anyway. Why even have conversations? Why not do a keg stand?

"So you're single, then?" he asks.

"Single-ish," she says. "It's complicated. Sometimes I feel like a stray cat, you know? I show up when it suits me. And you think I'm only eating at your house, but I'm eating at every house on the block."

"You're weird," he says. He wraps his body around her in a hug that feels more like strangulation.

"I'm quirky," she says. "There's a difference."

"I gotta ask you, though, the jean jacket and Birkenstocks and shit. Be real with me. Are you a lesbian?"

She wiggles her way out of his grasp. "Another total misread."

"What the fuck is going on over here?" one of the guys interjects, grinning like a maniac. He's lanky and bespectacled and drunk in a euphoric way. Not Al Pacino, but she can work with it.

"Your friend is sloppy as hell, and being kind of mean," Quinn says. She ignores the look of betrayal from the first man and gives Contestant #2 doe-eyes. "Are you here to save me?"

Before he can answer, Jessica slides in and puts her arm around Quinn. "This is our new friend Aaron," she says. "Look at his finger before you start acting like a freak. He's married."

7:46pm EST

Just as she has done for the past several nights, Rosie pours merlot into a sippy cup and screws the lid tight. It's not pathetic, she tells herself, it's *genius*. It's the only way to avoid shattered glass and stains suggesting homicide on her Turkish kilim rug.

One's home should be pristine, not a crime scene! Is this funny? Should she write some of this down? Tips like these would be great for her mommy blog, if she could ever get it going, if she could just lay off on the wine for one night.

She scoops up Henry and takes him into the den, where the two of them collapse onto the sofa and he squirms out of her grip, tumbling across the cushions and toppling pillows like Godzilla on a bender. Rosie nurses her drink and opens her laptop, which is useless because it's almost bath-time and then bedtime and then story-time and then typically a full hour passes and she's singing him Talking Heads songs and they're making funny faces and the only person feeling remotely sleepy is her.

There's no way Rosie could have predicted the current landscape of her life: granite countertops, stainless steel appliances, luxury vehicle,

Cincinnati, Ohio. She couldn't have predicted that a city with *sin* featured twice in its name could be so mundane.

But the main thing she never could have predicted is Henry. Don't get her wrong; Henry is the light of her life. He is three, with a perpetual fruit-punch mustache and a tendency to adorably trip and fall, even when he's just walking. Nevertheless, Henry is the reason she left the workforce and has not yet found the motivation to return. Henry is the reason she is fifteen pounds past her goal weight and four years behind her peers.

Back in college at Brown, she always imagined that at thirty she'd be single, childless, and likely living in Brooklyn. She craved an existence both austere and invigorating—long periods of solitude punctuated by moments of artistic breakthrough. She wanted overpriced cocktails in dimly lit bars and men that drifted in and out of her life in the same way her professors did, staying just long enough to make an impact, praising her and teaching her and then disappearing into the recesses of memory for good. But none of this happened! She graduated and let the inevitable anticlimax creep in. Moved back to Cranston and waited tables and waited for life to happen to her.

Somehow, now eight years later, something that *could* be called life has happened to her, and it isn't right. Her copywriting career started and sputtered, she met a man in a bar who became her husband, had an extravagant wedding that cost more money than her parents' salaries combined. The irony of his job title, anesthesiologist, is not lost on her; from the moment they married it felt like she'd been gently nudged into slumber, encouraging her to sleepwalk through life guilt-free.

On paper it all looks fantastic. In reality, she wears drawstring pants and guzzles merlot from a sippy cup. It is eight p.m. and she does not know where her husband is. It is eight p.m. and she has a ghoulish red-wine smile and a toddler at her feet, asking *where is daddy where is daddy* on a loop.

"Daddy is in Las Vegas," Rosie tells him, for what must be the hundredth time.

"Lost Vegas," he replies.

5:55pm PST

Quinn and Aaron are people-watching.

"I treat people-watching as a competitive sport," she says as they sit on one of the plush velvet loveseats that line the wall. "Sometimes I'll stare at a man and a woman and think, *daughter or second wife?* But in Vegas, the answer is usually *third wife.*"

They eye a flock of girls in stilettos and devil horns tugging at their short dresses as they scoot past. "The way the girls dress here," Aaron says, shaking his head in disapproval. "It almost eliminates the need for the strip club."

"Almost," she says.

"I don't get it. I mean, a girl can dress how you dress and still be super hot."

Quinn hopes this is a compliment. "Well, let's not judge them," she says. "Maybe they just want to look pretty for their date rape."

"Jesus," he says.

"Too real for you?"

"Just real enough. You're brutally honest."

She smiles and takes a deep slurp of her drink, her third. "The world is a dark, shitty place. It calls for dark, shitty people."

Her friends are all laughing now, at something totally separate. Something about the coffee scene in Seattle? She can't pick up on their conversation, nor does she want to. Their lack of cynicism is not easy for her. She has to be on her best behavior around them, and her best behavior is on par with most people's worst.

"I don't think you're dark or shitty," he says. "I think you're cool."

"That's very sweet of you," she says.

He laughs at her, strangely. He is so *on.* His energy hasn't waned since she first shook his hand. "You must be impervious to compliments at this point," he says to her. "You're gorgeous, you're funny, you're confident, and you're like, *I know, I know, I know.*"

Quinn rolls her eyes. "Being cool is the worst," she says, and he laughs at her in total disbelief. "No, really. I would give anything to be uncool. And to, like, feel happiness without having to feel so jaded all the time. To actually smile for once, instead of all this smirking."

As she speaks, she notices he is giving her this look now that's a combination of a lot of things—like he wants to hug her and help her but also maybe fuck her. She's not sure. But he is married. And it makes her feel weird. Weirder than usual.

"So is that a real wedding ring?" Quinn asks him, reaching for his finger. "Or is this all just a charade to make you seem forbidden and sexy?"

"I'm not sure how effective that strategy would be. I am definitely married."

"For how long?"

"Five years."

"Any kiddos?"

"Yes, one kiddo," he says. "He's three. He's hilarious. He's so smart and so curious about everything. He's at that great age where everything is new, you know?"

"I do know," Quinn says, though she can't recall the last time she was around a three-year-old. To Quinn, three drinks in, in Las Vegas in this hotel bar, the thought of a child is preposterous. "Okay, so what do you do for money?"

"For money? You mean, like my job? This is turning into such an interview. Like, where do you see yourself in five years?"

"Where *do* you see yourself in five years?" Quinn asks. "And be honest. Don't say 'prison.' That's what everybody says." She notices his hand is on her knee now, thumbing the blond hairs she missed while shaving. He is past the point of disguising his attraction. He is making it beyond clear, and her friends are too drunk to notice.

"Why don't you guess my job?" he asks. "This will be fun."

"I don't know. You're a consultant. You do some masturbatory job that makes no sense to me. Something with ideas and money."

"Wrong. I work in a hospital. I save people's *lives*, damn it!"

"I'm sorry I underestimated you," she says, grinning. "So you're a doctor?"

"Anesthesiologist," he says.

"Did you bring any powerful sedatives to Vegas?"

"Oh, definitely. Barbiturates, benzodiazepines… I've got Bill Cosby's medicine cabinet up in my hotel room right now."

"Wow," Quinn deadpans. "You really know how to get a girl excited."

"Yeah?" he asks, his hand crawling up her thigh. He is joking, being creepy for the sake of being funny, but just the quick contact has her tingling a little, and she has to exhale carefully to make the feeling pass. "Do you want to come up to my room and check it out?"

Quinn tries to read him—is he fucking kidding? Isn't he fucking married? She realizes no one, not one person she's met since she arrived at McCarran the previous day, has asked her what *she* does for a living.

"Sure," she says. "Why not?"

9:00pm EST

Rosie knows you are really not supposed to drink while on antibiotics. But who's going to rat her out, her toddler?

That morning, she leafed through pamphlets at her OBGYN, smugly judging the various ailments and infections that irresponsible people have to endure. Her pregnancy with Henry had been complication-free, much like the rest of her life. Being married was so easy! All the existential stress that plagued her young adulthood had dissipated—she was comfortable, she was happy, she was loved. She pictured herself wrapped in a cocoon of good vibes, good vibes she could pass along to the receptionist and the nurses and all the poor schmucks in the waiting room. But when the UTI test she had expected to come back positive came back negative, her doctor suggested they run a few more.

"That's not really necessary," Rosie said. "I'm married."

"I know you are," her doctor assured her. "This could be a bacterial infection. It's very important we check it out, just for peace of mind."

And so Rosie squirmed on the paper lining of the examination table until her doctor returned and offered her the uncomfortable word *chlamydia*, and told Rosie she was not there to judge, that this was pretty standard and that she was lucky to catch it in time because most people who have it don't experience symptoms and become vulnerable to pelvic inflammatory disease and even infertility, so, if anything, this is *good* news.

"Don't cry," her doctor said. "This is relatively easy. You just need to take a course of antibiotics for seven days. Really, I see this all the time.

There's zero judgment if you or your partner did something to jeopardize your reproductive health."

"Oh, I'm judging the hell out of him," Rosie said, and then wept alone in her doctor's office for half an hour until she became a deconstructed version of herself, all head in hands and hands slick with tears and tears staining the collar of her blouse. She cried until she was nobody's wife, cried until Ohio was gone and she was twenty-two in Narragansett at the mouth of the Atlantic, wondering if she'd ever find love like spackling, a love to patch up all the gaps and cracks in her personality, a love to fix everything that was wrong with her. At that time, she had felt so wounded, and worse, so alone with herself. That kind of aloneness was mind-fucking. That kind of aloneness kept her crying in the doctor's office until she was asked to make room for another patient.

As she tucks Henry into bed, she wonders what the point of the cocoon has been. Has it totally deadened her senses to the blaringly obvious? As far as she can see, there have been no signs pointing to infidelity. This is a man who races through the house with his son hoisted onto his shoulder, a goofy, sometimes awkward man who makes her laugh and makes her think and takes her to Acapulco sometimes, just because. But does "just because" stem from guilt? Is every kind gesture a reflex of his conscience recognizing that he's done a bad, bad thing?

This is all too much for Rosie to swallow. She wants to vomit, wants to call him and sob into the receiver until he apologizes and promises to change, but she knows he won't answer. It's three hours earlier in Las Vegas, which means he could just now be sitting down to dinner, or he could just now be sitting down in a strip club, or some strange woman could be sitting on his lap. If she calls, who knows what he would tell her? She thinks it would be a lie.

7:14pm PST

Quinn feels like a stereotype, fucking a married man in a city like this, a city whose entire premise is about reveling in indiscretion. He bats at her breasts and she leans down to kiss him, vaguely disappointed about getting what she wanted. All the banter, the flirting, the tension, it is all such a tired formula at this point, leading like clockwork to this moment. And yet she loves the attention! She can't get enough of it. She's like an animal, begging for someone to throw more meat into her cage, desperate to feed her starving ego.

"*God*, you're hot," he tells her, and she insists he say it again.

The curtains are drawn, but the room is bright. For most people in Vegas, the night is just getting started. She moves on top of him, hoping one of them will come soon. She tries to think about how sexy this man is, how tall he is, how much money he makes. They have chemistry, maybe. They share a sense of humor. She tries to think of these things, and tries not to think of his marriage.

"What's wrong?" he asks. She turns her head away, but he turns it back. "Hey, you don't seem into this."

Her own infidelity has always felt like a badge of honor, like that she's some kind of badass free agent and the rules do not apply to her. But she wonders about people who *do* want to follow the rules. Is it fair to disrupt their order?

Or is trying to impose order a total waste of time?

There is suddenly noise in the next room—the slamming of keys on a counter, the heavy click of the front door. His friends. "No man, those girls were fucking lame," someone says.

"Is that door locked?" Quinn asks, still on top of him, and before he can respond Brad the Bachelor flings it open.

"Jesus, Aaron," he says, and covers his eyes. The rest of the guys flock to the doorway, drawn to the commotion, and Quinn sighs. She hops off of him and tries to bury herself in the sheets.

"This shit again?" someone asks. There's a chorus of rowdy disapproval and disappointment, none of it sounding that serious, and they close the door. "Use protection!" someone hollers, and she wonders if that would have been a good idea.

"Will you just come on me?" she asks, but he gets out of bed and slips into his boxers.

He fidgets around the room, visibly shaken by the interruption, searching for something to do with his hands. "I'm sorry that was kind of a bummer."

"You do this a lot?" she asks. She wishes she had a cigarette to light—it feels appropriate.

"Come to Las Vegas, or...?"

"No, *this*. Your friends don't seem too blown away."

"It's complicated," he says. "You don't know my situation."

"I mean, I think I do. Your wife is boring because she bore your child, right? She hit thirty and you decided she was too old, because you're like, I don't know, thirty-five and want to be dating twenty-two year olds."

He crosses his arms. "What's with the armchair psychology?"

She pulls the covers up around her. "I'm just telling it like it is. I mean, I don't think there's anything inherently *bad* about cheating on your wife. The way I see it, what you don't know can't hurt you, right? I'm assuming you feel the same way."

He looks around for the rest of his clothes. "I don't really think about it at all."

"Oh, please."

"No, really," he says. He picks her denim jacket up off the floor and thrusts it toward her. "If you're not doing anything later and you want to get fucked again, you know where to find me. If you want to start in on a bunch of judgmental bullshit, I'd recommend finding someone else. I know that won't be hard for you."

"Geez," she says, and begins the demoralizing process of sliding back into her clothing, item by item. "I thought I was supposedly so cool."

"You were cool until you weren't. I don't know what else to tell you. I thought you were different."

Quinn picks her purse off the ground. "I see how it is," she says. "You thought I was different because I'm easygoing, right? Because I say the right things, because I'm agreeable, because I'm opinionated without having any opinions that threaten you. But you don't want to put up with the shit that's a little less convenient, do you? You don't want me to say anything you don't want to hear."

"Well, I'm sorry you're disappointed that I don't want anything more than sex from you right now. But to be fair, I never offered you anything more. And the fact that you're more upset about that than sleeping with a married person says a lot about you."

"I thought we weren't analyzing each other," Quinn says.

"We're not. You don't need it because you already have yourself all figured out. You know what you want and you know how to get it." He stares at his bare feet and rakes his fingers through his hair, clearly exasperated that she's still even there at all. " I don't get how you can expect anyone to take you seriously. You don't take yourself seriously at all."

Out of habit, Quinn rolls her eyes. Maybe it's to keep herself from crying. "Thanks for enlightening me," she says, and opens the bedroom door.

She makes a point to look at each of the men on the way out, assuming they've heard everything, refusing to give them the walk of shame she knows they want. They are slack-jawed, their expressions untrained, like they've all just been slapped.

Quinn, to her credit, is shameless.

10:40pm EST

From their bedroom, Rosie texts him: "You will need to schedule a doctor's appointment. ASAP."

She expects hours to pass, but she sees him typing. The expectation builds, and then: a question mark. He could call her, but he doesn't.

"Las Vegas is a shit show," he writes a moment later. "Pointless without you."

She smiles despite herself and cradles the phone to her chest, imagining it's him: the liar, the cheat, the deceiver, the imposter husband. What would it be like to start from scratch without him, at this point? What would it be like to be alone? At least he is somebody, she thinks. At least he is a living, breathing human who chose her all those years ago, even if the whole thing was a fraud. At least he truly loves Henry.

She lifts the layers of bedding and crawls into bed with him, slumbering and snug and curled up like a cat under the covers. She studies his face—the tiny upturned nose and the dark, thick lashes that make him look just like his father. Someday his hairline will recede. He'll gray at the temples. He will tower over her and she will shrink. As a young man living under her roof, he will date, sleep with girls, stand them up, break their hearts. She will be complicit in all of this, because she loves him and, to her, he can do no wrong. She will turn a blind eye to the beer cans in his car, his nefarious browser history, condoms on the bedside table, stains on the sheets. She'll hold her tongue to criticize him, because he was and is and will always be her baby, and because she knows he'll act blameless in the face of his fuck-ups, just like his father.

8:11pm PST

Quinn, somehow, is lost again.

So she wanders claustrophobic down the hotel corridors, dizzied by the carpet patterns. The doors to the rooms are closed, but she can easily envision who is behind each one: a bachelorette believing her marriage will unspool before her without kinks, a couple convinced their meet-cute is so much more adorable and amusing than anyone else's, everyone assuming that they will be spared the horrors that befall other people. Did Quinn think *she* was the exception, crawling into bed with Aaron? Did she think he saw something in her and wanted to reward her for playing along so well, for being such a good sport? Who was she kidding, it had nothing to do with who she was. She could have been anybody.

A thread of denial stitches together every single person in this hotel, she thinks. Maybe everyone in the whole goddamn city. She wonders what the point of any of it is—the quest for love, homeownership, stick-figure family on the back of the minivan and a dog in the backyard. She could invest years and years of good behavior only to be confronted by infidelity both surprising and inevitable, like a parking ticket on her windshield that forces her to ask *why me? Did I deserve this? I guess I deserved this, didn't I?*

She knows her friends, if she could find them, would tell her she is being fatalistic. Surely love has been lurking somewhere in all those dorm rooms and frat houses and hotel bars, waiting to reveal itself to her. It would be easier to give in to wanting all the things that women are supposed to want. Keep a positive outlook, they would tell her, chin up. If the world is a dark shitty place, maybe the last thing it needs is her dark, shitty attitude.

Through the wall she hears familiar female fussing, the din of a hypothetical argument, laughter that cuts through the chaos like an avalanche. Quinn presses her ear to the door and confirms it. It's where she's supposed to be... isn't it? She knows that if she's honest with her friends, it reveals she's been fucked too long by life to believe in love, they will envelop her in an embrace that feels corporate somehow, that reeks of Girl Scout Camp or a twelve-step program, and will tell her, "But *we* love you, Quinn," as if that is enough.

CAMERON MORSE

BABY BASICS

Centerpoint Medical Center: lower conference room
9:11 p.m.

A nurse shoves the head of her infant into a hinge
of hip bones, the pelvis in her hands

spring-loaded, the mouth
of a bear trap.

Demonstrating descent, she jams its rubber head
into the jaws and it crowns,

the way we are born, every one of us, slipping
bloody into the light of this world.

REMEMBER THE
ECLIPSE, BABY?

This sonnet meant to capture the eclipse
refuses to behave or get in line.
It's like those glasses that you had to grip
with both your hands to keep from going blind.
I'd hoped this fancy format would provide
much needed oomph and lift to elevate
my theme. Some better verses hide
just out of sight in lines I can't create.

But what did I expect? A moment filled
with awe and tears and hugs, totality,
sublime surrender, air begins to chill—
who dares to write on that reality?
It can't be done. But that's okay. And so maybe
I'm just saying, "Remember the eclipse, baby?"

GROCERY LIST

The clean shaven professor—
educated at Bowdoin he shyly confessed—
told us how hard it is to
define *literature*, how
it's easier to know what it isn't
than what it is.

And the students all agreed
that a grocery list
certainly is not literature.

But the list you are writing, my dear,
would give that earnest professor pause.
Here is an economy of language and
a structure charting a choreography
from aisle to aisle without retracing a step
because time is of the essence
when you bring kids grocery shopping.
And I see the imagery of green peppers,
fire-roasted canned tomatoes,
and extra-sharp Vermont cheddar cheese.

At the kitchen table
you imagined then composed then revised
seven breakfasts, seven lunches,
seven dinners each multiplied by four—
a text hiding the law of its composition
and the rules of its game.

ORIGAMI

I suppose these folded paper figures must go.
They've been perched, drooping, on my dresser
for three weeks with no signs of doing anything
other than blending in with the loose change
and receipts, which are also fairly useless.

But I don't want to scoop up the yellow
and purple butterfly,
the flapping-bird-of-happiness, the lotus flower,
and the slightly crooked T-rex
and drop them in the wastepaper basket.

If I do, they'll have to slug it out
with the tissues and sticky lollipop
sticks until I empty the trash
and then they'll make the uncomfortable
trip in the back of a garbage truck
to the dump, a fate too cruel.

And if I do it, I'll be relying
on memory to hold on to the three
days in June when I folded
dozens of them for my kids.
Now which one should we do?
We'd flip through pages to find a good one
and then detach along perforated lines
the right piece of colorful paper in
the back of the book.

Can I count on myself to remember it?
I feel safer with objects to touch,
and the next batch of temporary mementos
will be arriving on my dresser soon.

CATCHING A CHICKEN

The movies make it look harder
than it is: Rocky Balboa dashes
breathlessly swiping and missing
at a hen, his trainer holding a
stopwatch berating him
through the montage until
the dramatic successful catch—
that kind of thing.

Catching a chicken, I learned, has
little to do with aerobics.
Rather than a boxer training,
a Zen master—stooped and calm
waiting for the chicken to come to him
then grasping in the nick of time—
would be a better candidate
for chicken catching.

Perhaps a poet would be up to
the task: a lake country Romantic
gazing out over a tarn waiting
for inspiration to strike and
then in an instant grabbing his pen
like so many tail-feathers
and scribbling across his page
emotions recollected in tranquility.

CONTRIBUTORS

CLAIRE COBURN received her BFA in Writing, Literature, and Publishing from Emerson College in Boston. Her short fiction has previously been featured in *The Adirondack Review* and *After Happy Hour Review*. She lives and works in the San Francisco Bay Area.

LINDA ELFERS-MABLI taught university-level writing and literature courses for over thirty years, both in the classroom and online. After years of encouraging her students to express themselves poetically, she is finally working toward an MFA in poetry and sharing her own work. She lives in northern New Jersey.

DANIEL GLEASON lives in Dayton, TN where he teaches literature, composition, and creative writing at Bryan College. He and his wife, Kathleen, have two young sons.

KEN HAAS lives in San Francisco where he works in healthcare and sponsors a poetry writing program at the UCSF Children's Hospital. His poems have appeared in over 50 journals, including *Clare*, *Freshwater*, *Helix*, *Natural Bridge*, *Nimrod*, *Poet Lore*, *Quiddity* and *Spoon River*. You can visit him online at http://kenhaas.org.

BRANDON MARLON is a Canadian-Israeli writer. He received his B.A. in Drama & English from the University of Toronto and his M.A. in English from the University of Victoria. His poetry was awarded the Harry Hoyt Lacey Prize in Poetry (Fall 2015), and his writing has been published in 200+ publications in 27 countries. brandonmarlon.com.

CAMERON MORSE taught and studied in China. Diagnosed with a brain tumor in 2014, he is currently a third-year MFA candidate at UMKC and lives with his wife, Lili, and newborn son Theodore Ian in Blue Springs, Missouri. His poems have been or will be published in over 50 different magazines, including *New Letters*, *Bridge Eight*, *South Dakota Review*, *Fourth & Sycamore* and *TYPO*. His first collection, *Fall Risk*, is coming out in January from Glass Lyre Press.

LISA TADDEO is a 2017 recipient of The Pushcart Prize. She received her MFA in fiction as the Saul Bellow Fellow from Boston University. Her fiction has been published in *The New England Review*, *The Sun Magazine* and *Esquire*, among others. Her nonfiction has been published in *Esquire*, *New York Magazine*, *Elle Magazine*, *The New York Observer*, *Glamour Magazine* and *The Sun Magazine*. Lisa's work has been included in *Best American Sports Writing* and *Best American Political Writing*. She is the winner of the William Holodnok fiction prize and the winner of the 2017 Florence Engel Randall Award in fiction. Lisa is currently at work on her debut nonfiction for Simon and Schuster, and her first novel.